Stolen Wonders

David Gatward ✱ Jonatronix

OXFORD
UNIVERSITY PRESS

HILL VIEW
JUNIOR SCHOOL
QUEEN ALEXANDRA ROAD
SUNDERLAND

HIGHLY CONFIDENTIAL

```
From:     STING, Charles
To:       Top secret
```
```
Subject: TEAM X
```
```
📎 Villain profile: the Collector
```

To *******

Following the arrest of Dr X, we have made several changes at NICE.

- NICE is now the *National Institute for the Conservation of Earth*.
- Dani Day has been appointed to the position of Senior Scientist.
- The mission of NICE is to help protect the planet and the precious things in it.

In order to help NICE in its mission, Dani Day has employed a team of four agents. She assures me that they are highly capable. In order to protect the agents, their real identities must remain a secret. They have been given the name Team X. Their operation status is now **code green**.

Team X have been monitoring a new villain. He calls himself the Collector. The Collector is known to have carried out some serious crimes [see file attached].

I will keep you informed of any further changes.

Regards

Charles I. Sting
Director of Operations, NICE

Important
Agent Information
Read this first

Villain profile: the Collector

Threat category: High

Known crimes:

- Theft of the entire population of cod in the North Atlantic.
- Theft of the White Cliffs of Dover.
- Theft of weather phenomena including four tornadoes. He found himself blown away, though, when he unwittingly released the extreme weather conditions.

Appearance:

Dark hair. Brown eyes. 182 centimetres tall. Snappy dresser. Bionic hand. Spectrum retina-enhanced implant.

Profile:

The Collector is a billionaire. How he made his fortune is not known. His goal is to own the biggest collection of snow globes in the world. Using advanced micro science and his most prized asset, the Master-bot, he shrinks and steals valuable objects. No target is too big. He does not care about the consequences of his actions.

Other things to note:

He likes to send snow globes to taunt his victims.

TEAM X DESTINATIONS

Destination: Wiltshire
Date: 3100 BC
Ancient wonder: Stonehenge

Stonehenge was built in stages between 3100 BC and 1600 BC. No one knows who built Stonehenge, or why. Also, no one really knows how the stones were transported over vast distances, or how they were stood in the ground with even larger stones placed on top.

Country: Polynesia
Destination: Easter Island
Date: AD 5100
Ancient wonder: The Moai

The Moai are huge human figures carved out of stone. They were carved by the people of Rapu Nui, also known as Easter Island, between AD 1500 and 1600. There are 887 statues in total, the heaviest of which weighs 86 tonnes.

Country: Egypt
Destination: Giza
Date: 2560 BC
Ancient wonder: The Great Pyramid

The Great Pyramid is the oldest and largest pyramid at Giza. It was completed in 2560 BC but nobody knows exactly how it was made. It is believed that it was built as a tomb for Pharaoh Khufu.

Chapter 1 – Stonehenge

Rising out of the ground, as though trying to touch the star-speckled night sky, the great rocks of Stonehenge stood silently before the security guard. As part of a team responsible for looking after the ancient monument, he made sure the rocks were protected at all times.

The guard flashed his torch up and down every stone, pausing at the largest and most imposing one. The huge rock weighed over 50 tonnes. It amazed him how people living 4000 years ago had been able to move something so enormous. Some stones had travelled over 200 miles, pulled on wooden rollers by hundreds of people.

The guard's radio buzzed. "Hi John," he said, holding down a little button on the side of the radio. "Everything's fine here. Nice and quiet."

"Great," replied the security guard at the other end of the line. "All quiet here, too. Perfect night for it, isn't it? Have you *seen* the stars? The sky is so clear!"

The guard dragged his eyes away from Stonehenge and looked up. Above him, a million bright specks of light pierced the night's inky sky.

It really was a beautiful place. He recognized some of the constellations, including his favourite, Orion, or 'the Archer' as he liked to call it.

The security guard shook himself out of his reverie. Something was wrong. For a moment he couldn't work out what it was. Then the realization hit him – Stonehenge had disappeared!

"John! It's gone!" said the guard, his voice shaking. "Stonehenge has disappeared! It's vanished!"

"What are you talking about?" John replied.

"Stonehenge!" said the guard. "It's gone! It's not there any more! It was and now it isn't!"

The guard walked forward into the space that, only moments ago, had been occupied by the ancient stone circle. He scratched his head, looking all around him. Where had it gone? How did something so large and so heavy just disappear?

"No, I mean," said John, "what's Stonehenge? Never heard of it."

The guard stared for a moment at his radio, almost as though he couldn't believe what his colleague had just said.

"What do you mean?" he answered. "It's what we guard, remember? Big stones? A place of huge historical importance?"

"No idea what you're talking about," John answered. "The stars are pretty tonight though, aren't they?"

The guard opened his mouth to reply, then paused. He knew that he had meant to say something, that it had been very important, but what it was exactly, he couldn't say. And why on earth was he standing in the middle of an empty field? How very odd.

"John?" said the guard, speaking again into his radio.

"Yes?"

"Put the kettle on. I need some strong tea."

With that, the guard walked across the empty field, wondering why he had been there at all.

Chapter 2 – Disappearing wonders

At NICE headquarters, Team X were staring at a dome clasped in Dani Day's hands. It was another snow globe.

"What's in it this time?" asked Tiger, leaning forward to have a closer look.

Inside was a strange collection of stones arranged in a circle. None of them had seen anything like it before.

"Let's have a look," said Max, reaching for the globe. "I wonder what the message is this time."

Max turned the globe over and there, on the bottom, was a message from their arch-enemy, the Collector; he always left a cryptic note on the bottom of the snow globes.

So many wonders, so little time!
Stolen, then forgotten,
and all will be mine!

"What does *that* mean?" asked Tiger.

"It means," said Cat, "that the Collector is up to his usual tricks!"

Dani walked over to the NICE computer and began tapping away at the keyboard. "I'm going to run a search to try and find out what those stones are," she said.

"Let's take a photo and use that," suggested Ant. "It might narrow the search a bit." Dani uploaded the image and the NICE computer whirred into life – the search had begun.

As they waited for the photo to upload, Ant started to think: something was niggling at the back of his mind. *The Collector always steals valuable objects*, he thought, *and those stones definitely look like the kind of thing that would be famous the world over. So why has no one seen them before and what does the clue mean?*

Ant shook his head, the answers evading him. He decided to do what he always did when a problem puzzled him: he reached for his favourite book, which at that point in time was *Wonders of the Ancient World*. He began to read. Maybe, just maybe, the answer would come to him.

Meanwhile, on an island far, far away …
The Collector was standing on a small, grass-covered cliff, looking out at the Pacific Ocean. Waves danced over each other, breaking into bright sprays of white bubbling foam. Hovering beside him was his Master-bot, a robot so powerful it could shrink absolutely anything and trap it in a snow globe.

The Collector looked to his right. Tilting his head upwards, he gazed at the rather large reason he had decided to visit this remote island.

Huge stone statues towered over him, each of them carved by many human hands.

"You will be a wonderful addition to my latest collection," said the Collector. A sinister grin danced across his face. "You know, I think I have outdone myself this time," he continued. "This could quite possibly be the perfect crime – no one will miss a thing! That is if my calculations are correct, of course, and my new invention works; but when have I ever been wrong? I just need confirmation … ah, there we have it."

Out at sea, the Collector spotted a small boat bobbing on the waves. He looked closely – it wasn't a modern boat, but a canoe, paddled by half a dozen men. The Collector's grin grew even wider.

"My time-travel machine," he said, clenching a fist with triumph, "*works!*"

The men on the boat stared up at the Collector high above them on the cliff. He hadn't been there moments ago. It was as if he had simply appeared out of thin air!

"Now, it's time I added a bit more wonder to my collection," he chuckled gleefully. He looked up at the Master-bot and nodded.

A laser beam, as bright as the sun, burst out from the robot. It hit each statue and they disappeared!

The men in the boat looked on in terror. How could this be possible?

The Collector looked out to sea and grinned. His Master-bot hovered above him, holding a new snow globe that glinted in the sunlight. Trapped within were the Easter Island statues – the Moai had been lost from time forever.

The Collector lifted his left arm and as he did so a strange device caught the light. It was a tarnished silver cube, covered in tiny metal cogs.

The Collector flicked a red lever, which was poking out from the top of the box. Tick, whirr, click ... the cogs began to move. It sounded like a hundred clocks all being wound up at once.

The men in the boat continued to gaze, baffled. They shielded their eyes as a bright light burst out from the clifftop. When they looked up again, the man was gone.

Chapter 3 – Wiped from history

Search complete. No matches found, flashed the computer: there wasn't *anything* that matched the strange circle of stones in the snow globe.

Dani turned to the team. "We need to figure this out soon, Team X," she said. "Whatever the Collector is stealing must be important. We just need to figure out why …"

Ant was still engrossed in his book. A vague idea was flickering at the back of his mind. For some unknown reason he felt sure the answer lay in these pages.

He turned to a new chapter about a place called Easter Island. His eyes quickly skimmed the page but, when he was about halfway down, the strangest thing happened: the text and photographs on the page began to dissolve.

Ant quickly switched his watch to video function – he had to show the others what was happening. Maybe together, they could make sense of this mystery.

Ant ran over to the others, connected his watch to the computer and downloaded the film.

"You're not going to believe this!" he said, pressing 'Play'.

Everyone stared at the screen and watched in amazement as the content of the book disappeared before their eyes.

"And it's not just this page," he said, flicking through the book to reveal more blank pages. "It only seems to be affecting this book, though. I've checked others and they're all fine."

"I don't understand. How can text just *disappear* and why only in one book?" asked Cat.

Ant thought for a moment. *What's different about this book? And what's it got to do with the stone circle?*

Questions crowded his mind as he struggled to make sense of it all. "I just don't understand what my book about ancient wonders has got to do with an unusual stone ..."

Ant froze. It was like a lightning bolt had hit him.

"What is it, Ant?" asked Dani.

"I think I know what the Collector is up to but ... it just seems too outrageous, even for him," said Ant.

"So what is he up to?" asked Tiger, eager to get to the bottom of the mystery.

Ant looked at Team X and Dani. "I ... I want to test out my theory before I try to explain it."

"At least tell us what you think is going on," said Max.

"It just seems too improbable ... but it's the only answer I can think of," replied Ant, almost to himself.

Before Team X could ask any more questions, Ant turned to Dani. "We need to go to Easter Island ..." He paused. "And we need to set our watches for AD 1500."

Team X gasped, they rarely used the time-shift function on their watches. They knew that if they changed even the smallest thing in the past, it could alter the present and the future, too.

"You just have to trust me," said Ant, seeing the concern on his friends' faces. "We have to go – right now."

Dani typed in the coordinates for the X-gate and Team X turned their watches, setting the time coordinates. One by one, they leapt through the X-gate, the light of the teleporter swallowing them.

Chapter 4 – Mysterious markings

On Easter Island, the X-gate glittered and glimmered into existence. Crackles of energy danced around it, lighting the sky like firecrackers as Team X stepped through.

Ant looked around them. There were no statues in sight. He checked his watch. They were definitely in the right place and the right year. His theory was right.

Max, Cat and Tiger looked at Ant expectantly.

"I think the Collector is stealing ancient wonders," said Ant matter-of-factly.

"OK, but why did we have to travel back in time to figure that out?" asked Tiger.

"Because he's travelling back in time, stealing them before they're famous," replied Ant.

"So every time he steals one of these wonders, all records of them disappear, too?" asked Max.

"Exactly! He's wiping them from history," said Ant. "Trouble is, I don't know what he's going to take next."

"Right," said Max decisively. "We need to look for clues to his next target. Let's spread out."

"Over there!" Cat shouted after a couple of minutes scanning the area with her magni-beam. "There's something caught in the bush."

Cat dashed over and carefully pulled the object free. It was a piece of coarse paper that looked very old. Written on it were strange markings and symbols.

"Can I have a look?" asked Ant, joining Cat.

Cat held the paper out and they both pored over it. Ant recognized the markings and the material immediately.

"It's papyrus," said Ant. "The markings are hieroglyphs." He pulled out his book on ancient wonders again. "Look, the same symbols appear on the Great Pyramid."

"Is that the next target?" asked Tiger.

"Maybe," answered Ant. "We don't have anything *else* to go on."

"Giza it is then," said Tiger, secretly hoping that they might meet a pharaoh.

Max hastily contacted Dani using the hologram function on his watch. "We need to go to Ancient Egypt, Dani. Reset the X-gate coordinates!"

"What …" started Dani.

"No time to explain, I'm afraid. We've only just missed the Collector. We don't want to miss him again!" Max said, switching off the hologram.

"To 2561 BC," called Ant. "Let's go!"

With that, Ant, followed by Max, Cat and Tiger, turned his watch and leapt once more through the X-gate.

Chapter 5 – The Great Pyramid

Team X found themselves in bright sunshine, walking on soft desert sand. A towering pyramid loomed over them.

"Wow!" said Tiger, squinting, trying to see to the very top of the giant structure. "It's huge!"

"We've travelled back in time approximately 4600 years," said Ant, working out the age of the pyramid from his book. "The pyramid itself took 20 years to build. It's nearly 150 metres tall – hard to believe it was built by hand, isn't it?"

"Did you just read that book, or swallow it, too?" asked Cat, with a smile.

"I think we might need a little help to cover ground," said Ant, gesturing at the vast expanse of desert stretching out all around them. A small bronze-coloured craft glinted in his hand as he pulled it from his rucksack.

"Hawkwing!" said Tiger excitedly. "Good thinking!"

Max, Cat, Ant and Tiger turned the dials on their watches, shrank to micro-size and climbed on board.

Max, piloting the craft, circled the Great Pyramid, which jutted up out of the desert like a great, gold tooth. Close by were a number of other, smaller pyramids. They seemed to huddle at the feet of the Great Pyramid like scared servants.

Cat stared hard at the pyramids as Team X flew round them but she saw no sign at all of the Collector.

"The Collector is definitely not outside the Great Pyramid," she said. "We're going to have to look inside. Take us down, Max."

Max carefully steered Hawkwing in close to the Great Pyramid and landed the craft, its engines sending clouds of sand into the air. Cat clambered out, grew to normal size and raced off to search for a way in.

"Wait for us, Cat!" Max called out, as he and the others grew to normal size and followed, eager to catch up with Cat. "We need to be careful!"

Cat stopped and turned to face them.

"I'm fine!" she shouted. "Come on! I think I can see a crack …"

The air around the pyramid started to shimmer.

"What's happening?" said Tiger.

Ant spotted it first, a dot in the sky, a bright beam emanating from it. "Oh no! The Master-bot! The Collector's trying to steal the Great Pyramid," cried Tiger, "and Cat is …"

Before Tiger could finish his sentence, the pyramid and Cat vanished.

Chapter 6 – Search and rescue

Max jabbed at his watch. "Dani? Come in, Dani! This is Max! We have an emergency!"

"Max! What's happened?" replied Dani, unable to keep the panic out of her voice.

"It's Cat," Max said. "The Master-bot has taken the Great Pyramid. Cat was caught in its beam and she's disappeared, too!"

"Oh no!" Dani fell quiet. She knew she had to figure out a way to find Cat but how?

"I've got it!" Dani called into the communicator. "Cat's watch can track your watches so we *might* be able to reverse the signal and use it to track Cat."

Dani ran her fingers across the keyboard of the NICE computer. She managed to pick up a very faint signal. It wasn't much but it would have to do.

"I think I've located Cat," Dani said, after what seemed like a very long wait. "The signal is very faint, though. I *think* she might be deep underground."

"Maybe the Collector has a new secret lair?" suggested Tiger.

"Get back to the X-gate," said Dani. "I'll reroute it to lock on to the signal from Cat's watch. It's a long shot but, if I'm right, it should get you close to her current location."

"I hope you're right," said Tiger. "Knowing our luck, we'll probably land on the Collector instead!"

Max and Ant didn't like to admit it but they were worried too – what if they couldn't save Cat? What would happen then?

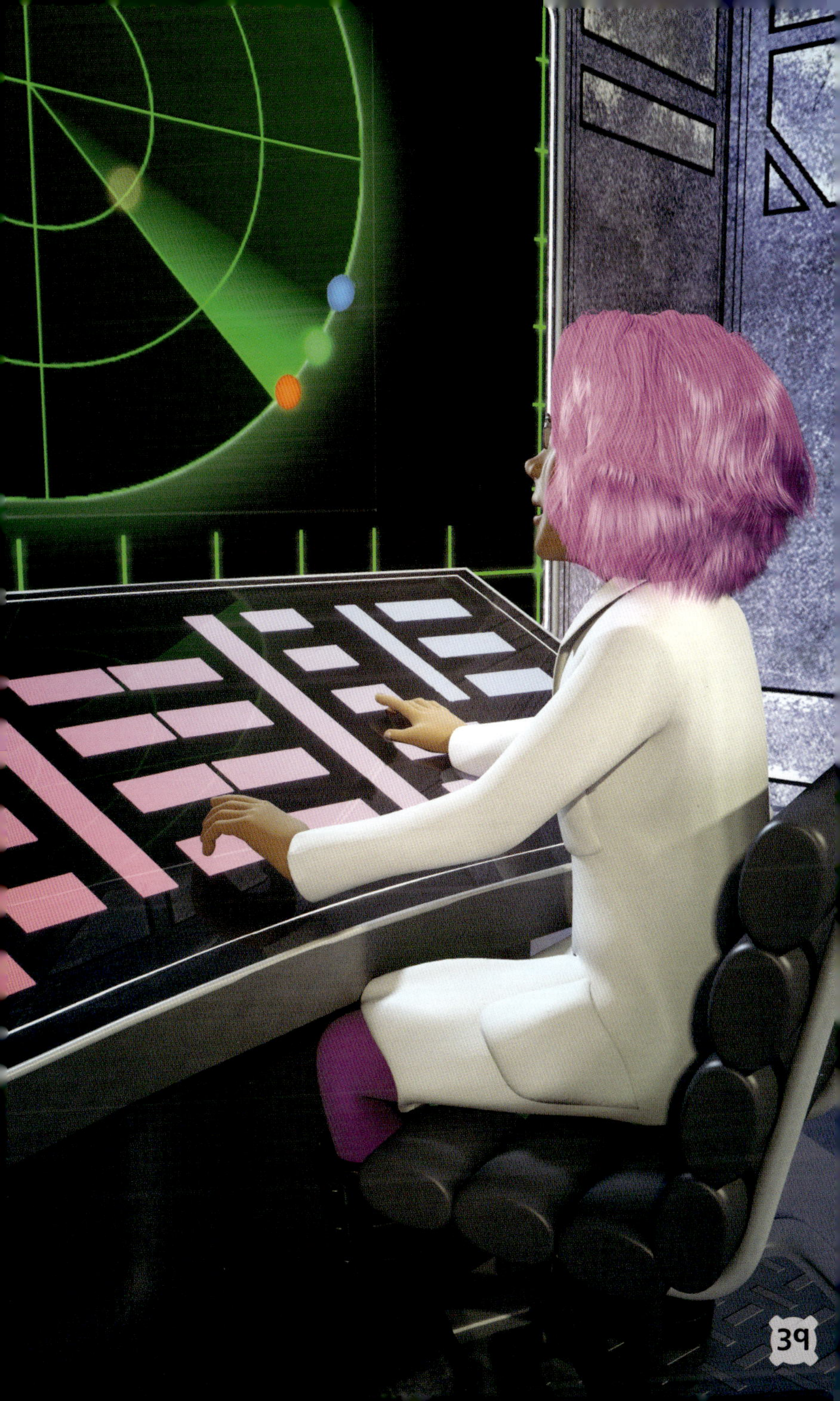

The friends looked at each other. They were Team X. They would complete their mission, no matter what – and with that, they raced through the X-gate.

41

Chapter 7 – Secret hideout

"It's pitch black!" Tiger gasped. "I can't even see my hand in front of my face! Where *are* we?"

"Dani said she thought Cat might be underground," said Ant. "Well, it looks as if she was right. Turn on your torch, Tiger."

Tiger pressed a button on his watch and a bright beam of light pierced through the darkness. They *were* underground – in a cavern so huge the beam of light couldn't illuminate the roof.

"Look," said Ant, pointing towards the furthest wall of the cavern. "Shine the light over there, Tiger."

The cave wall in front of them looked as if it had been chipped away many years ago.

"I think we're in some kind of ancient mine," whispered Ant. "It's the perfect hideout for the Collector!"

The blue shimmer of a hologram appeared from Max's watch.

"Cat isn't far away now," Dani said. "In fact, judging by the signal I have here, she's almost right in front of you."

Ant edged forward. "It's just a solid wall, though," he said.

Tiger shone his torch along the chipped stone and the light revealed a tunnel at the far end of the wall, stretching away into the darkness.

Max, Ant and Tiger crept down the twisting tunnel. After only a couple of seconds, it opened up into another cavern; this one was well lit, with a desk, a chair and a number of tarpaulin-covered boxes in it. They blinked, their eyes unaccustomed to the brightness after the gloom of the tunnel.

Something glinted in the far corner of the cavern. As they drew closer, a carefully aligned row of pristine snow globes came into view with ancient buildings trapped in some, while others were empty, waiting to be filled. A flicker of movement caught Ant's eye. He looked towards one of the globes and there, standing in front of a pyramid-shaped building, was Cat!

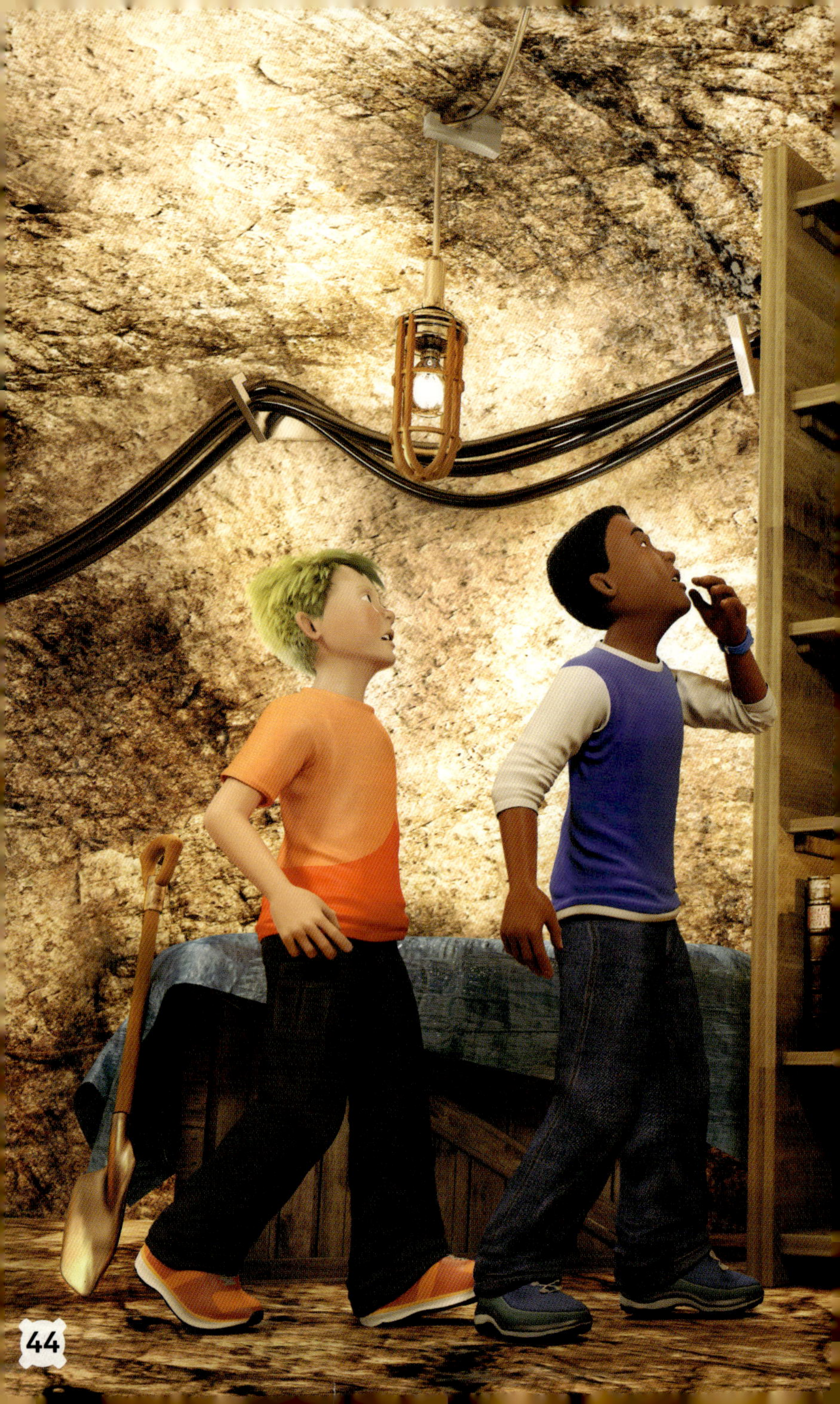

45

Chapter 8 – Great escape

"Cat's trapped!" cried Tiger. "What are we going to do?"

"Well, we can't break the globe to rescue her," said Max, sounding more calm than he felt. "If we do that, we'll be crushed down here!"

Ant started pacing round the room, desperately trying to think of a solution.

"We need to grab all of the snow globes and get out of here," said Tiger.

"But what about the Collector?" asked Ant. "He'll just steal more and more things; who knows what damage that will do? He could change history forever."

"We need to find his time machine and fast," said Max. "Spread out and scour this place. I'll check the shelves."

Max dragged a crate over, clambered up and started looking behind each of the globes. As he reached up to the top shelf, he noticed an odd cube perched at the very top. A lever jutted out – Max strained to grab hold of it, his fingers brushing the edge of the cool metal. Just then, they heard footsteps approaching. All three froze.

"It's the Collector! Quick, you two, shrink and hide!" Max whispered. "I've almost got it."

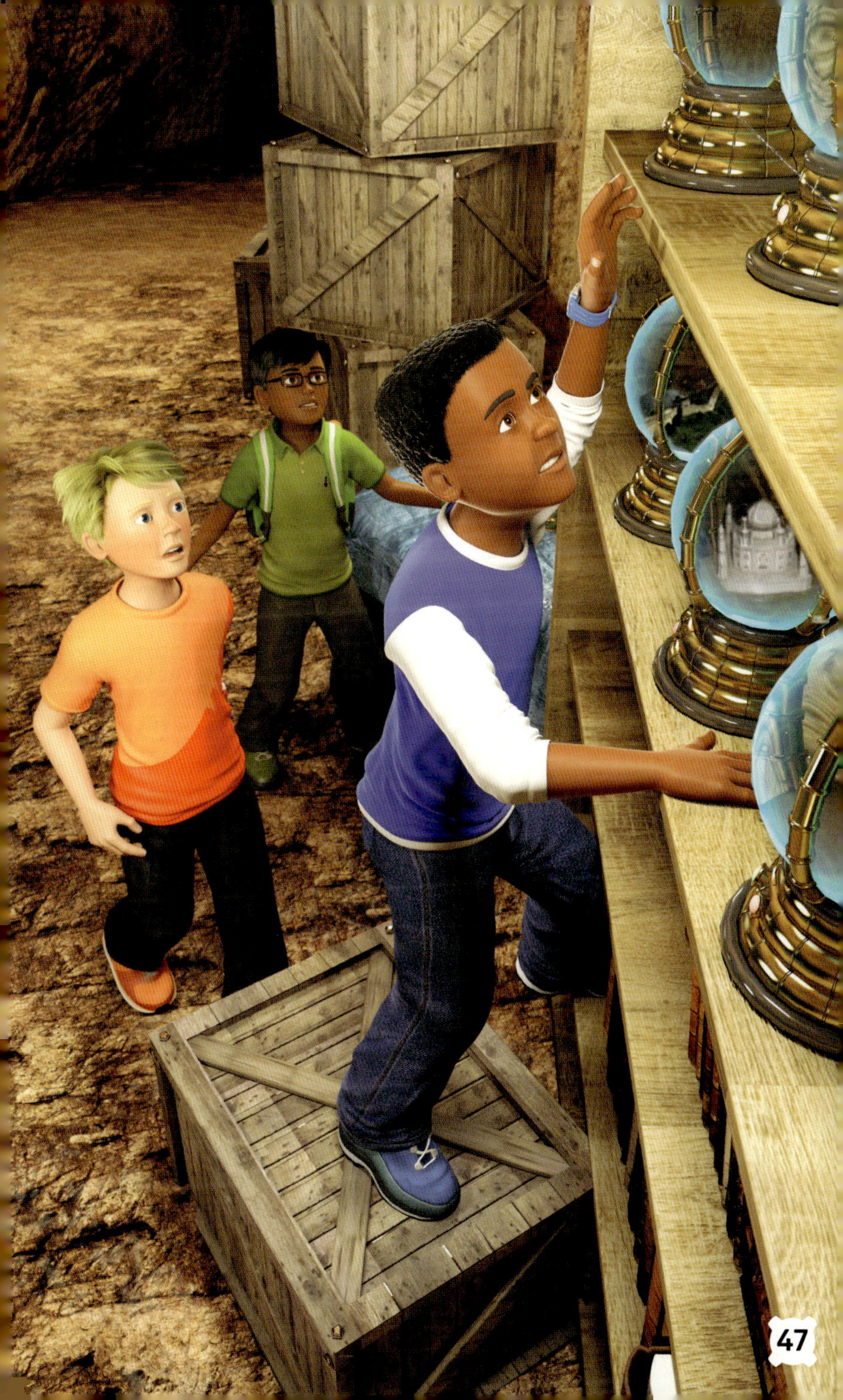

Max teased the cube off the shelf but couldn't reach Cat's globe in time. He dived behind a box just as the Collector entered the cave.

Max watched as their arch-enemy walked into the middle of the cavern, cradling a new snow globe in his arms.

"My plan is coming together perfectly," he said to himself. "Soon, the world will have no wonders left! Then I *wonder* what they'll do," he sniggered. "Now that I know it works, I can move on to part two of my fiendishly foul plan. It's time to shape the future; all I have to do is tinker with the past a little more. Now, where shall I ..."

The Collector stopped, fear momentarily rising within him. Then he smiled. "I see you've found my time machine," he said. "Do you really think you can stop me now?"

The Collector paused. Then he reached for a globe – Cat's globe. She cried out but no one could hear her.

"If you don't hand me back my machine," said the Collector, "then you will never see your little friend again!"

49

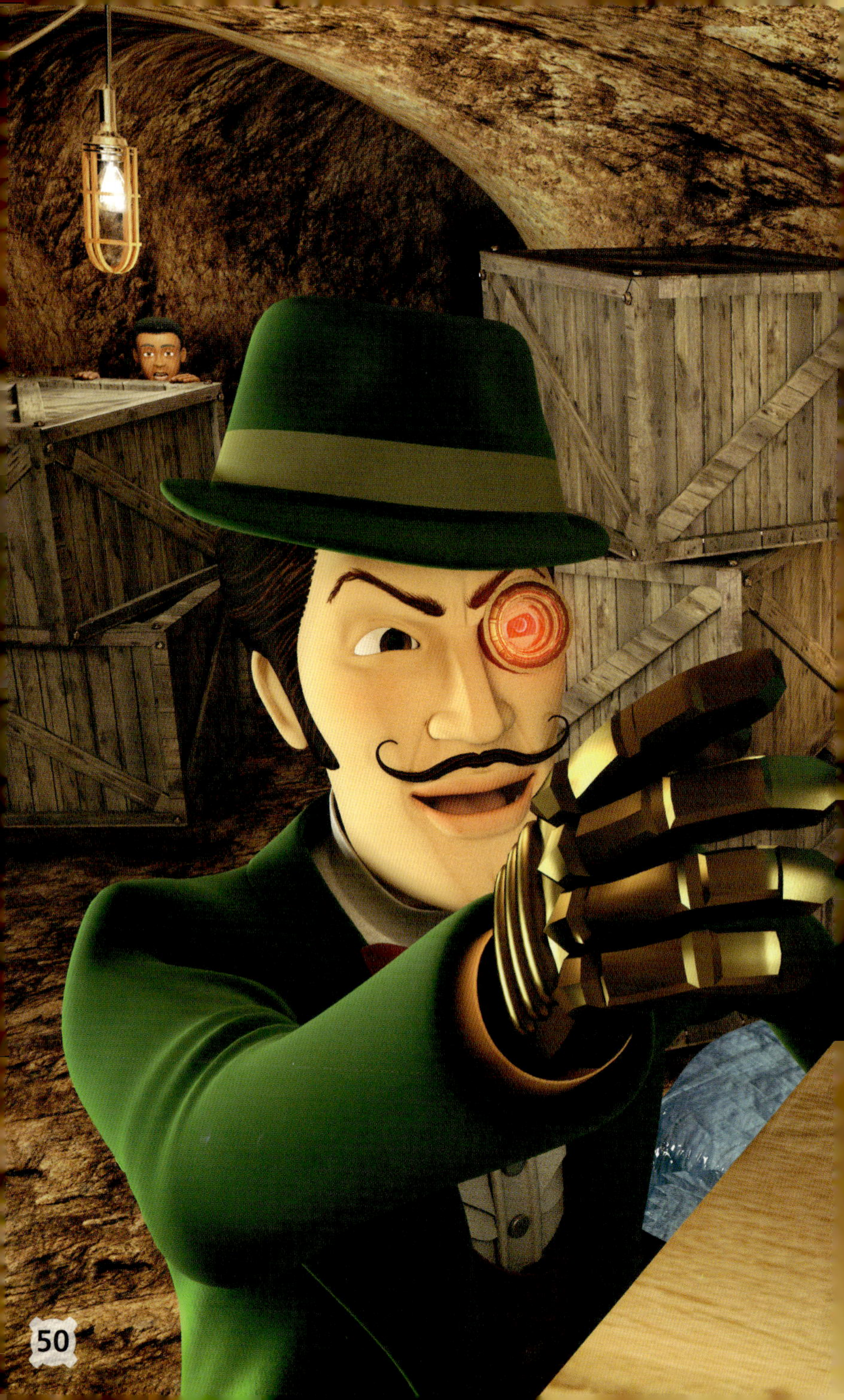

51

Ant and Tiger gasped as Max slipped out from behind the box. The silver cube, the Collector's precious time machine, was clutched in his hand.

"OK," said Max. "You can have it. Just put my friend down!"

The Collector smiled a sneering, arrogant smile: he was enjoying this.

"Of course," he said, placing Cat back on the shelf. "Now, the device?"

Max threw the cube high into the air. The Collector reached out and caught it – but his grin soon turned to a frown as around him the air started to shimmer and warp.

"You fool! What have you done?" the Collector cried.

Max raised his hand; in it was a small red lever. The Collector screamed – then vanished!

53

Chapter 9 – Wonders returned

Ant and Tiger ran out from their hiding place.

"Well done, Max," smiled Ant. "That was quick thinking."

"But he's escaped!" said Tiger.

"No, he hasn't," said Max. "I've sent him back in time. Who knows where he might be?"

Ant laughed but Tiger looked worried. "Won't he just come back?"

"Not without this," grinned Max, unfurling his hand to reveal the red lever. "I doubt the machine will work without it."

"Well, with the Collector out of the way, all we have to do now is set Cat free and return the wonders to their rightful homes. We just need to figure out where they belong," said Ant.

"*Just!*" smirked Tiger. "You make it sound so easy, Ant."

Ant smiled. "Easier than it might have been if the Collector had put the second part of his plan into action!"

"We need to return the pyramid first," said Max, looking at Cat, still micro-sized and trapped in the snow globe. "Otherwise she may never forgive us!"

55

"OK, Dani," said Max, as her hologram appeared before them. "We've found Cat and stopped the Collector. There's just one small problem. She's trapped in a globe with one of the wonders so we need to return to our previous location."

"Well done, guys. Setting the coordinates now," replied Dani.

The X-gate shimmered in the darkness ahead of them and Max, Ant and Tiger stepped through.

Seconds later, the three-friends walked out into the burning heat of the desert once again. Ant carefully placed the globe on the ground.

He turned to look at Max and Tiger: he was nervous about smashing the globe. What if it hurts Cat?

"It'll be OK," said Max, sounding more confident than he felt.

Ant picked up a stone and, very carefully, tapped the glass sphere.

A faint crack appeared, slowly spreading further down the glass towards the base.

Then, in a blinding white flash, the globe exploded, shattering all around. Max, Ant and Tiger hardly dared to look.

"And about time, too!" said Cat, now standing in front of her friends, smiling. Their eyes snapped open.

"Thank goodness you're safe!" cried Ant with relief.

"Look!" said Tiger, pointing behind Cat.

There, back in its rightful place, stood the pyramid.

Ant opened his book of ancient wonders. The picture of the Great Pyramid was back in its right place, too.

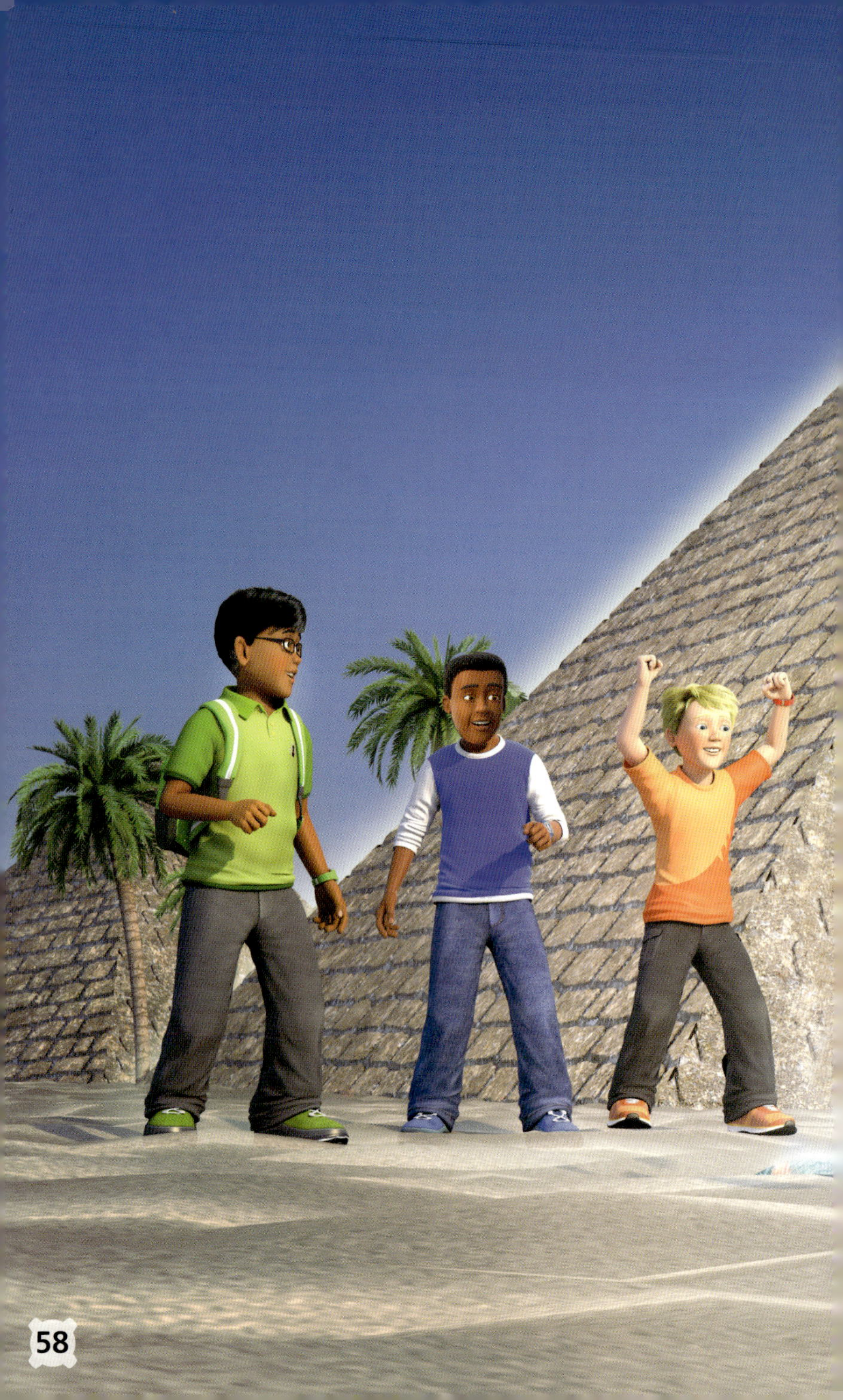

59

"So that's one down," said Cat. "How are we going to work out where the others belong?"

"We need to head back to the cave – I'm sure the Collector will have hidden detailed plans somewhere," said Ant.

"Right. Let's go," said Max, just as a hologram appeared from his watch.

It was Dani.

"I see you managed to free Cat. Well done, Team X. I knew you could do it," said Dani, sounding relieved. "Now, I hate to do this to you but I need you all back here at once, I'm afraid!"

"But we haven't returned the other wonders," said Max.

"Don't worry," replied Dani. "Remember that until they've been returned, no one actually knows they existed in the first place! I'm afraid I have a mission that is far more urgent. Hurry!"

With that, Dani's hologram vanished. Max, Cat, Ant and Tiger looked at each other.

"This sounds like a job for Team X," said Tiger, smiling.

A heartbeat later, Team X jumped through the X-gate and were gone.

NICE

HIGHLY CONFIDENTIAL

```
From:     STING, Charles
To:       Top secret
```
```
Subject: TEAM X, MISSION UPDATE
```

To *******

I would like to inform you that Team X have foiled the Collector's latest dastardly plan. We have been monitoring the Collector closely and had begun to suspect that he had developed his own time-travel technology. Our fears were realized when wonders of the ancient world started to disappear one by one.

If it had not been for the deductive skills and courage of Team X, the mystery of these disappearing treasures would have remained unsolved and the wonders lost forever. Furthermore, the Collector had plans to alter the future by meddling in the past.

Not only did Team X solve the mystery and rescue the stolen wonders, they also banished the Collector to Easter Island AD 1501. I doubt he will cause NICE any future problems.

Regards

Charles I. Sting
**Director of Operations,
NICE**

Meanwhile, on Easter Island AD 1500 …

Find out more ...

Learn how to become a detective and help solve a mystery in *A Super Sleuth's Manual*.

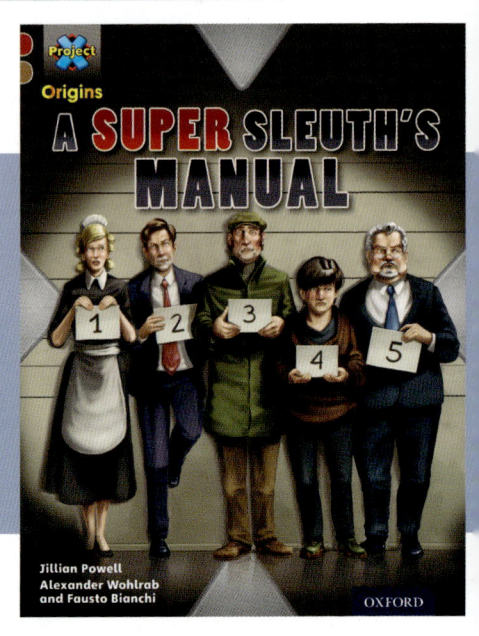

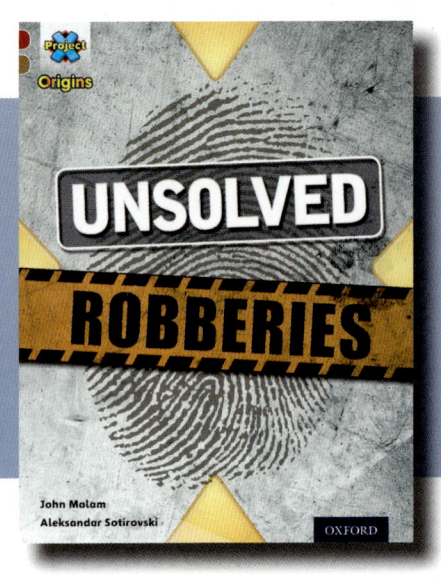

Find out about some of the world's most famous *Unsolved Robberies*.